ZOOM!

How to Win Right Now as an Operations Supervisor

John Thacker

MBA, LSSBB

Meridian Publishing
An Imprint of JB Enterprise LLC
Grand Prairie, TX
"Making the world a better place through knowledge"

Copyright © 2019 by John R. Thacker Jr. All rights reserved. Printed in the United States of America. Except as permitted under the United States Copyright Act of 1976, no part of this publication may be reproduced or distributed in any form or by any means, or stored in a database or retrieval system, without prior written permission of the publisher.

ISBN: 978-1-7343377-0-9

Library of Congress Cataloguing-in-Publication Data
Thacker, John
    ZOOM! How to Win Right Now as an Operations Supervisor / by John Thacker
      p. cm.
ISBN: 978-1-7343377-0-9 (alk. Paper)
   1.   Business. 2. Self-Help Methods. I. Title.

For Brenda

Your unflagging loyalty and faith in me

Cannot be separated from

Anything I am or do

CONTENTS

1. Leadership 101 — 1
    a. What Leadership Is
    b. Polish Your Strengths, Outsource Your Weaknesses
    c. Managing Up

2. The Four Pillars of Lean — 13
    a. Standard Work
    b. Leader Standard Work
    c. Visual Management
    d. Regular Accountability

3. Getting things Done — 31
    a. Three Methods for Getting Things Done
    b. Executing Your Deliverables
    c. Effective Delegation

4. Get Better Every Day — 41
    a. The Continuous Improvement Mindset
    b. Eliminating the Eight Wastes
    c. Measuring Outcomes and Limiting Reaction

5. Conflict Resolution — 55
    a. The Conflict Resolution Model
    b. Cognitive, Emotional, and Behavioral Elements
    c. What if They Just Say No

Introduction

Why did I write this book, and how will it benefit you? Well to be honest, every Supervisor I've ever hired struggled with some basic knowledge of how to be effective. And you know what? I struggled with these same things when I started. I've worked with some amazing companies with fantastic training platforms (Walmart) and business operating systems (Bosch, Honeywell), but apart from training internal to specific companies, I couldn't find a resource dedicated to helping first time salaried employees succeed. You see, I wasn't a great Supervisor myself. I've always pursued training, coaching, and knowledge to hone my skills – and it has been a challenge. So when I was first put in a position to bring on leaders and coach them, I looked for a few good resources. Of course, there are plenty of excellent books on leadership, organizational culture, and management. But that is not what I needed, and that is not what my Supervisors needed. There are five basic elements that all Supervisors need to be successful, and believe it or not, I couldn't find any books written to address this need. So I wrote one.

This book is intended to provide you with immediate knowledge as well as clear instruction on actions you can take right now to be successful – that is why I named it *ZOOM! How to Win Right Now as an Operations Supervisor*. It is fast, effective, and can be put into practice immediately. Each chapter has two or more subsections. These subsections describe an important concept, and then is followed by a "how to do it" section. These sections explain concrete actions you can do right now to implement change. Each chapter wraps up with a "chapter recap". The recap revisits all the key concepts in quick, one sentence definitions.

It is my sincere hope that you and others will use this book to improve your capabilities, value creation, and impact on the world and your community by "making the world a better place through knowledge".

ZOOM!

How to Win Right Now as an Operations Supervisor

Chapter 1

Leadership 101

What Leadership Is
Polish Your Strengths, Outsource Your Weaknesses
Managing Up

What Leadership Is

How is John F. Kennedy like George S. Patton? Patton was a rough-riding career officer, Olympian, and Army general with a potty-mouth. Kennedy, by contrast, was a soft-spoken, refined, career politician, and his WWII experience, while noteworthy, was as a Navy reservist commanding a solitary, 80-foot PT boat. So what do they have in common? Leadership. There is a very important lesson here – no one is born a leader, and there is *no such thing* as a perfect or "right" leadership style. This is pivotal, because frankly, a lot of people are scared by leadership. They think that being an effective leader requires the development of skills or attributes they don't possess, position or privilege that is unattainable, or having some kind of magic touch like Steve Jobs or Jeff Bezos. Rubbish. No one is born a leader, and there is nothing keeping you from being an effective, successful leader. Rather, all leaders have developed the skill of enlisting help from others. Leadership is commonly accepted as **"A process of social influence in which a person can enlist the aid and support of others in the accomplishment of a common task."** Let's break that definition down.

- Process

It is important to remember from the get-go that leadership is a *process*. There is no final destination where you can sit back and say, "I'm a leader!" In fact, not only is there no such thing as a natural-born leader, there is no such thing as a complete leader. Leadership is relative to context. Sometimes we confuse a "take charge" personality with leadership. In reality, a "take charge" personality can actually reduce your social influence, and inhibit your ability to lead. It can also make you do stupid things. Consider the CEO of a tech company who is very skilled at influencing those within her company to get things done. She is on her way home from work when there is a terrible car accident in front of her. Being a take-charge person, she jumps from the car, and immediately begins barking orders. There is only one problem here. She has no social influence in this situation, and the bystanders awkwardly ignore her. Some even start filming the event on their phones. Social influence is a *process*. Anyone can jump in and start barking orders, but that doesn't make you a leader, and it doesn't always work. Take the time to form relationships with your team. Take the time to create an environment where relationships can be leveraged.

What's the lesson here? Leadership isn't about your personality or your position – so stop worrying about those things! You received everything you need to be an effective leader the moment you were born. Instead of worrying about things you can't change very well, focus on the process of influencing others.

- Social Influence

Consider this Arab proverb. A young prince was leading his band of merry men through the unforgiving desert. Being young and a bit insecure, he was quick to direct even the smallest of tasks. The problem was that the Prince didn't really know what he was doing – he was "faking it to make it". Now there was an older, wiser attendant that had served the king before the prince, and he saw what was happening. He didn't say anything to the Prince. He didn't contradict him, he didn't challenge his authority, and he didn't point out when the Prince was making questionable decisions. Instead, he quietly made suggestions to the Prince. He was careful to do this in a casual way, out of the earshot of the other travelers. In this way, he preserved the Prince's honor. The Prince, for his part, was completely oblivious to the man's methods, but it worked. In this manner, the wise old servant saved the entire caravan. This proverb is a great example of what real leadership is. The Prince had positional authority, but lacked the wisdom to admit his limits and seek inputs from those with more knowledge. The servant, on the other hand, lacked any kind of positional authority, but leveraged social influence to ensure the entire caravan arrived safely at their destination. The true leader of the caravan was the attendant, not the Prince.

This is an important leadership lesson. Positional authority is not the same as leadership. Just because you're a Supervisor doesn't mean you have social influence, and just because you aren't doesn't mean you don't! Remember, at the end of the day, all you can ever *really* do is influence others. Even dictators can't force people to do things. If they could, humans never would have invented torture. Frankly, bad leadership has a lot of common elements with torture – both inflict pain in an attempt to change behaviors. Don't be a terrorist. Use positive social influence to effect change.

- Enlist aid and support

This is the crux of leadership – you are enlisting the aid and support of others. Keeping this in mind is the key to being effective. A leader does not want drones or worker bees. A leader does not see people as things. A leader understands that he or she is responsible for making a vision clear, but that the leader can't do it without others. Enlisting aid and support requires knowing what your team's strengths and weaknesses are – which requires knowing your team. You can't be an effective leader without taking the time to form relationships with your team. So what if this isn't your strong suit? Don't worry about that. Think of your employees like a valuable asset. If you owned a race horse, you would take the time to know what it was capable of – does it race better on cinder or dirt? Rain or shine? Quarter mile or half? You can't win a race if you don't know what your horse is good at. In the same way, you have to know what your team members are good at. Even if you aren't very good at forming relationships, that doesn't mean you can't talk to your team and find out what they are good at and what they want to get out of their work experience.

- Accomplishment of a common task

This one should be self-evident, but often it isn't. Leadership requires a common task. It needs to be common – everyone working on the same thing – and it needs to be a task – a concrete deliverable rather than a vision or idea. There are two things you need to avoid here – first, avoid having *too many* tasks to work on. In fact, the fewer tasks, the better your team will perform. This is because any kind of task requires *new* actions, ideas, and deliverables. New means *change*, and people frankly don't do well with change. So be careful to avoid the "five Cs" – Continual Change Creates Constant Confusion. The other thing you need to avoid here is not having a *task* for your team to accomplish. This idea is a little more dynamic, because the level of abstraction in task delegation increases the higher one moves in an organization. For example, as an Operations Supervisor, you need to give your team a concrete task – we are going to fulfill this many orders, with this many labor hours, by following this standard work. On the other hand, a CEO will give much more abstract tasks to his team – the CFO, for example, might be tasked with reducing the firm's CUR by 5%.

How to do it

- *Keep a work journal*

First, every idea in this book can be helped greatly by simply keeping a work journal. This notebook should be on your person at all times. You'll want to take personal notes in here, so use one small enough to fit in your pocket – you don't want to leave it laying around where anyone can look at it.

- *Learn your employees' names*

This is a key component of building social capital. Use this simple trick to remember your employees' names. Introduce yourself and ask them what their name is. Immediately select one aspect about them that sticks out in your mind – it might be their hairstyle, accent, or wardrobe. Say a few pleasant sentences to them, and repeat their name three times. Every time you say their name, imagine that unique characteristic in your mind. For example, you might say something like the following:

"Hi, I'm Stacy, your new boss; what's your name?"
"I'm Jaterrick."
{Jaterrick is wearing a purple shirt. Jaterrick is the purple shirt guy.}
"Hi Jaterrick," *{first mention of name; imagines purple shirt}* "It's a pleasure to meet you."
"So Jeterrick," *{Second mention of name; imagines purple shirt}* "How long have you been doing this job?"
"Oh, about four years." *{Makes mental note to follow up with this employee as he may have insight into the business}*
"Nice! I'd like to talk to you later about your experience. It was a pleasure to meet you, Jaterrick." *{Third mention of name; imagines purple shirt}*
Once you leave, you may choose to write down the employee's name, what their job is, and the purple shirt.

- *Learn your employees' skills and desires*

This is fairly easy to do – everyone likes to talk about themselves. The key here is to learn what your employees are good at – so you can use them skillfully – and to learn what they want to get out of work – so you can motivate them. Write what you learn down in your notebook.

> **Where the Rubber Meets the Road**
>
> *Each section of this book includes a "how to do it" section. These sections suggest practical action that you can take right now to see greater success!*

Polish your strengths, outsource your weaknesses

So you just got your review, and your boss tells you that you need to "work on" something. I hate to break it to you, but your boss may be dead wrong. Consider this – we all come in a multitude of different sizes, shapes, and colors. So why wouldn't we all be different on the inside? Consider a young man in high school. He is very athletic and plays two sports, but he can't hit a curve ball. What should he do? Well, his coach might tell him to stand in the batting cage and hit at curveballs all day, all summer. That might work. A little bit. For a while. The better coach tells the young man to have fun playing baseball, but to work on his basketball skills instead where he is already succeeding. The young man listens to this advice and goes on to become a professional basketball player. That is a true story. Think about it this way – imagine that you have a skill that you are very good at, in fact, you are in the ninety-fifth percentile. Now imagine that you have skill that you just aren't very good at. You are in the tenth percentile in this skill. Which skill should you improve? Well, if you work six months to improve your better skill by 4%, you are now one of the best in the world at that skill – a fact that you can leverage financially and professionally. But if you spend those same six months to improve your bad skill by 4% you are still bad at it! So spend time improving your skills, not your weaknesses.

Now that doesn't mean you can ignore your weaknesses – far from it. You need to be very aware of your weaknesses, and this is where that performance review can come in handy. But the secret to rapidly achieving efficiency as a leader is not to work on your weaknesses, but rather to be aware of them and to control them. The best way to do this is to outsource your weaknesses. Think about it this way: your firm probably has accountants. Now why is that? Well, simply put, the operational leaders in your firm aren't good enough at it! Instead of trying to do something they are not very good at, they outsource it to someone who is. So take some time to jot down notes on what you are not good at, and then jot down how you can control that weakness or outsource the task you are not good at.

How to Do It

- *Seek feedback*

Your organization probably already has an avenue for you to get some feedback, be it a performance review, one-one-one or 360 feedback. You can also solicit feedback from your direct reports and your peers. Try to keep this simple and drama-free. For example, you might distribute an online or paper survey, or just talk to people and ask them, "What am I good at?" "What can I work on?" Sometimes people are apprehensive about feedback – don't be! Everyone is allowed their opinion, and it might help you quite a bit. New leaders especially can be concerned about image, especially in organizations where new leaders are turned over very quickly. Often, you might feel the need to defend yourself. Try to avoid this impulse – it tends to have a dampening effect on feedback and isn't very healthy for you either. Try to listen respectfully to all feedback, even if you disagree. Think about the times you provided upward feedback – how did you want your boss to respond?

- *Sort your feedback*

Arrange your feedback in categories, and select *one* strength to work on and *one* weakness to control. These should probably be the ones that people mention the most.

- *Do your strengths; outsource your weaknesses*

If you keep getting the feedback that you are good at talking to people but maybe not so good at reporting metrics, then you should probably do the shift startup meeting with your folks, but recruit a team lead or subject matter expert (SME) to do your reports for you.

_____

Managing Up

This is probably the topic that I get asked about the most – how do you manage your boss? The fact is that you and your boss don't see eye to eye, as a matter of human existence. People are different. Don't assume that she understands you or that you understand her. It doesn't work that way. Instead, you have to take an active role in managing your boss. That's right – leadership goes both directions. Remember our definition of leadership? A process of social influence to enlist aid in a common task…and your boss is not only fair game to influence, but might be the most help of all!

If you keep a few basic ideas in mind, it will help you to enlist the aid and support of your boss as you pursue business excellence and success. First, keep in mind our definition of leadership – enlisting aid and support. Now consider that your boss is trying to enlist *your* aid and support in accomplishing a common task. One way to keep things professional no matter how you *feel* about your boss is to always consider your boss your number one customer. Having this mindset will allow you to look past petty irritants and "keep your eye on the prize". Of course, it also helps if you are able to disagree in a way that is neutral and respectful. If your boss is even a little bit good at his job, he expects you to disagree and voice those concerns.

To be honest with you, I am not a huge fan of the term "managing up". The truth is, working with your boss is not primarily a factor of *management*, but of *relationship*. You should be striving for a healthy, positive relationship with your boss. It is a unique kind of relationship, to be sure, but it is primarily relational, rather than transactional. This brings us back once again to our definition of leadership – leveraging social influence to enlist aid in the accomplishment of a common task. This is a fundamentally relational definition, and working with your boss is no different.

How to Do It

- *Anticipate your boss's needs*

Take notes every time you talk to your boss, especially in the first few months. What do they keep mentioning? What do they complain about? What do they ask for help with? If you can find a pattern, you will identify your boss's *values*. This will allow you to anticipate your boss's needs. It is always better if your boss doesn't have to ask every time she wants something.

- *Understand your boss's motivation*

What is your boss good at? What is he bad at? What does she enjoy doing – or hate to do? What motivates your boss? Again, take notes with this specific question in mind. The goal here is to conform your actions to your boss's preferences. If she loves giving group presentations, invite her to do so. If he hates monthly accounting reports, volunteer to do this for him.

- *Know how to talk to your boss*

I don't mean that you need to be on eggshells here, but rather that you are going to have to bring problems to your boss – that is part of their job description. But there are probably plenty of others bringing their problems to your boss as well. So take some time to think about how you go about it. Make sure that you have a suggested solution for every problem you bring, and don't get hurt feelings if your boss goes another direction.

- *Be a helper*

Your boss is paying you to solve problems, so always orient your actions around making your boss's life easier. Write down a few ways you can make their life easier.

_____

Chapter One Recap

Leadership is: "a process of social influence in which a person can enlist the aid and support of others in the accomplishment of a common task".

Leadership requires: Social influence, delegation, clear communication

Strengths are: Activities, actions, or skills that you perform better than most of your peers

Strengths should be: Put to good and frequent use

Weaknesses are: Activities, actions, or skills that most of your peers perform better than you

Weaknesses should be: Known to you, controlled, and outsourced

Managing up is: The process of leveraging social influence to enlist the aid and support of your boss

Things to Remember

Each chapter in this book ends with a "chapter recap". This section includes brief bullet points of the major concepts found in this book. Use this section to review, refresh, or even memorize key concepts that you have learned.

Chapter 2

The Four Pillars of Lean

Standard Work
Leader Standard Work
Visual Management
Regular Accountability

Standard Work

Lean is one of those industry jargon words that you will have to be familiar with in operations management. Everyone is familiar with Lean for manufacturing, but these days Lean is applied to everything from hospitals to call centers. Chances are you've heard words like "5S", "Kaizen", and "muda". In this book we will not get into all this jargon (really...how can Lean be Lean if you have to learn a new language to talk about it?); rather, we will look at the four things without which you won't be able to run a Lean operation. This is intended to just give you the basic understanding you need to be successful, make good choices, and speak intelligently to your peers and superiors.

Standard work refers to having one way of performing a certain task that everyone follows. That is why it is called "standard work". Standard work is probably the most important part of running your operation because it creates consistency and establishes a baseline from which improvements to the process can be made. Here is a good example of how important standard work is and how it is essential for you to run a clean operation. Imagine a "quick-lube" service station that is in the business of providing 15 minute "while you wait" oil changes. This business has standard work – every time the oil is changed, the service technician replaces the filter, then replaces the drain plug, then fills the engine with oil. After this, a second tech checks the filter and drain plug torque, starts the vehicle, and observes for leaks and oil pressure. Because the work is performed the same way every time, it protects the customer from having their engine damaged, and ensures that the work will be done in about 15 minutes. Now imagine the same business without standard work. The technician knows what to do, but does it differently from time to time. One day he forgets to tighten the drain plug, and the second technician is too busy adjusting air pressure in the tires to perform his check. The oil slowly drains from the engine, and half way home, the customer's

car burns up. What a disastrous result! The lesson is clear – doing a task the same way every time allows for consistent results – and consistency is the key to running a good business. Consider for a moment the fast food industry. No one gets a fast food burger for a fine dining experience. But because the burger consistently tastes the same way, for the same price, with the same wait time, people buy millions of fast food burgers per day. The way to have a successful fast food restaurant is to be consistent, not to produce the best possible food. That is why dollar menus are so successful.

In the same way, you need *consistent* execution and outcomes from your team. This highlights a problem sometimes associated with standard work. Sometimes, some organizations use this term as a euphemism for a written document. In actuality, standard work is cultural – it is a mindset rather than a tool. Plenty of organizations have reams of written documents, but their team members don't necessarily follow them. Sometimes this is because the documents are unclear or poorly written. Sometimes it is because the documents haven't been updated to keep up with changing work environments. And sometimes this occurs because the leaders of the organization haven't cared to develop the culture of standard work.

Don't misunderstand – having a written standard work document is an essential part of having standard work. It is the tool that gets everyone on the same page and sets the standard for how things should be being done right now. However, without constant communication and attention to culture, the documents will not mean anything. Standard work documents are tools that have to be used.

How to do it

- *Learn your processes*

The first step to having standard work is to know what processes you are responsible for. This is where your work notebook can come in handy again. Write down what you own. Now go learn it. Work with your employees and do as much of the work yourself as you can. Ask questions and let the employees know that you are relying on them to help you be a good supervisor.

- *Document the best way you know how to execute your processes*

This can be as simple as a series of hand written bullet points, but each step needs to be outlined in order. For example, your document for "Making a Peanut Butter and Jelly Sandwich" might be as simple as the following:

- Gather ingredients
- Apply peanut butter to one slice of bread
- Apply jelly to the other slice of bread
- Close bread
- Cut in half
- Wipe down working surface

Later on you can begin to add in details to the process, but even this basic structure allows a significant level of consistency. For example, consider how different the outcome might be if one of your employees was cutting the bread in half prior to applying the peanut butter and jelly.

- *Train your employees*

Use the document you just created to train all your employees on "the one way" that we are going to do a job. At this point you should expect some push back from employees who have better or more clever ways of doing the work. When this happens, you can acknowledge that some of your employees likely do have some really good ideas that we can incorporate later in revisions, but that starting from a single, consistent way of doing things is crucial to the success of the operation. You'll want to encourage ideas and improvements, while also making sure everyone is clear that the team needs to be compliant with whatever one process is currently released.

- *Examine the results*

Don't forget this crucial step! You absolutely must schedule time *every day* to watch your employees work and to examine their outputs. When you watch them work, track their actions against the document you just created. You want to ensure they are following the standard work. When you inspect the output, you are ensuring that the process is resulting in what you actually want. For example, after watching someone follow the standard work for "Making a Peanut Butter and Jelly Sandwich", you may discover that the finished sandwich is soggy. After investigating a bit, you realize that this is a result of using too much water when wiping off the work surface. This is an opportunity to update the standard work with clarifying instructions.

Leader Standard Work

Hamadi just got promoted to Supervisor, and he is excited about the opportunity. He comes to work and on his very first day is bombarded with requests from his boss, his peers, and his employees. Eager to make a good first impression, he tries to get it all done. While he isn't able to accomplish everything, he goes home satisfied at his ability to address issues and make a good first impression. Unfortunately, when he comes in to work the next day, his boss points out that his team forgot to execute an important project, and that certain business goals or metrics were not met.
Hamadi is crestfallen! He was trying his best, but lost sight of the critical components of running his business. Does this sound familiar? Thankfully, there is a Lean tool that can help you avoid these kinds of pitfalls.

Your employees need to perform the same work the same way every day in order to get consistent results – and so do you! Thankfully, Lean has a tool to help you perform consistently as well. Leader Standard Work, or LSW, is a document that outlines what you and your Team Leads need to be doing every day. If Hamadi had been using an LSW, he would have ensured that his project got done, and that his important metrics were being executed. The idea here is to automate the decision-making process – this reduces "decision fatigue" and allows you to ensure that the important things get done every day. If your company has a Lean BOS (Business Operating System) then you may just be given an LSW to use. If so, congratulations! You'll want someone to explain it to you, but your life just got a lot easier. If you're like almost everyone else, however, you will have to make your own LSW. Don't worry, it isn't too difficult, and we don't have to get too deep into Lean management theory to write and use an effective LSW. Basically, your LSW is a checklist of things that you have to do every day to run your business. Why is this a fundamental pillar of Lean? Well, simply put, we want consistency. Your LSW is the management version of the Standard Work we looked at in the previous section. Your LSW should list the minimum set of tasks that you must accomplish every day to run a consistent business.

How to do it

- *Log a week's worth of work days*

First, use your work journal to track everything you do for one week. Additionally, you want to make special note of things that your boss asks you to do as well as requests and requirements from other stakeholders. Basically, you want to write down everything you do each day. Be sure to track what you did by specific day of the week, as you want to know what repetitive tasks you have.

- *Solve for the common tasks*

Now look at your journal and figure out what tasks you are doing every day. These need to go in your LSW. At some point (not necessarily in the beginning) you will want to add weekly and monthly tasks to your LSW.

- *Analyze your processes*

Of course, there is always the chance that you missed something, so take a few minutes to look at your process list from the Standard Work section, and figure out *what specific actions* you must take to ensure the processes are running well. This will include tracking performance on a production board or takt board, observing your employees daily, and participating in continuous improvement projects.

- *Build your Leader Standard Work*

List out the activities you must execute daily in order to ensure your processes are being executed well and returning valuable outcomes.

Here is a list of what a Supervisor LSW is likely to include:

Once a Day:
- Meet with previous shift ("handshake" meeting)
- Monitor shift startup (ensure all processes get started and are running)
- Lead Tier 2 meeting with team lead(s)
- Attend/contribute to Tier 3 meeting
- Complete assigned CI work
- Gemba walk with your team lead(s)
- Standard Work observation and audit (deep dive) one process
- Write out plan for next day
- Update your time-keeping software or system
- Meet with next shift ("handshake" meeting)

Throughout the Day:
- Department walkthroughs
  - Walkthroughs focus primarily on volume and aging of WIP, but should also focus on cleanliness, monitoring progress boards, and process adherence
- Review, initial progress boards; action as needed
  - This is the task of looking at how each process is executing as recorded on the progress board, initialing off, and initiating corrective action when outputs are out of tolerance
- Monitor team lead standard work
  - Your team lead(s) have their own standard work, and you are responsible to ensure it gets executed

> **What is WIP?**
> "WIP", a common industry term, stands for "work in progress". It refers to any work that is being worked on, but is not yet finished. Some WIP is physical, such as a pallet of goods that has been unloaded from a truck but not put away, while other WIP is digital, such as a customer complaint call that has been logged but not resolved yet.

Speaking of Team Lead standard work, your Team Lead(s) also need an LSW and chances are that you will be actively engaged in helping them write it. Your Team Lead's LSW should probably contain the following items:

Once a Day:
- Lead Tier 1 meeting
  - The "start of shift" meeting, which we will look at in depth a bit later, reviews the previous day's accomplishments and sets the direction for the current day's work.
- Review and adjust your labor plan
  - The Team Lead needs to know how many people came to work, and immediately escalate to you any staffing needs.
- Monitor shift start up
  - Getting the processes started and stable is a key component of what the Team Lead does.
- Post production numbers
  - The Team Lead is responsible for ensuring that the visual management tools are being used.
- Attend Tier 2 meeting
  - This is the venue for escalating staffing needs, etc.
- Complete improvement task assignments
  - Everyone in the organization has something to deliver to keep the organization moving in the direction of continuous improvement.

- *Write it out...and use it*

Ok, once you have done a little bit of research and note taking, just write it out – it can be as simple as the bullet points listed above. The way you use an LSW is pretty simple. Print it out and carry it with you at all times. Take your notes on it, note any employee interactions, and list process observations, etc. As you accomplish your tasks each day, just cross them off the list. Review your LSW and notes once per day and look for things you were supposed to do and didn't get done as well as things that weren't on your LSW that you had to get done. You may need to adjust your LSW. Also look for action item notes you took throughout the day that you need to close out. Keep in mind this basic idea about the LSW – if you do the tasks on your LSW every day, you may not be a super star, but your business won't fail. That is what you are going for.

_____

Leader Standard Work

Standard Work for: *Docks Supervisor*
Name: *Your Name Here*
Week Ending: _____

Daily Follow-up

	M	T	W	H	F	DONE
Shift alignment with OM						
Shift Handoff w/ opposite Supervisor (take pictures)						
Review carrier schedule with TL to plan						
Observe Tier 1 Meeting/Labor flex						
GEMBA walk						
Tier 3 Meeting						
Receiving Productivity Board/Repack status check						
Validate scanning by transporters in BTS						
Ultipro time check						
Everyone back in area from lunch						
Check Repack board every 4 hours						
Employee feedback/Thumbs-up or Think						
Receiving Productivity Board/Repack/Grief status check						
Audit TL LSW						
Shift Change Handover w/ 2nd						
Passdown meeting						
Observe No Fly						
5S						
Prepare topics for next day Tier 1 w/ TL						
Validate Pre-shift Inspections						
Prepare/Send the Shift Passdown						

Weekly Tasks:

- BBS observations
- Ohno circle
- Confirm orders for open positions
- Weekend OT plan communication
- Planning for next week's action items w/ TL

TASKS

Description	Status
	P D C A

CI PROJECTS

Description	Status
	P D C A

FOLLOW UP WITH EMPLOYEES

Description	Status
	P D C A

Flow Interrupters

Example

Visual Management

It will be pretty hard for you to Supervise if you don't know how your team is performing! Just as important, it will be difficult for your employees to do their best and succeed if they don't know how they are performing. Lean uses the term "Visual Management" to refer to the act of making your team's performance visible at a glance.

A common every day example of visual management is the dashboard on your car. By glancing at your dash, you can tell how fast you are going, how hard the engine is working (if you have a tachometer), what temperature the engine is at, battery charge level, etc. Most modern cars even show you the air pressure in your tires. Now imagine if you didn't have that dashboard – the only way to tell how fast you are going would be to measure the time elapsed between a known-distance landmark (such as telephone poles, which are 125 feet apart in urban areas and 300 feet apart in rural areas), and then do some fancy math to figure out how fast you are going. Needless to say, that method is far too difficult to be used frequently, and you will probably end up getting a speeding ticket!

In the same manner, a work "dashboard" makes the performance of your team visible so that you can assess performance and make corrections quickly. Generally speaking, you will want to limit what you are measuring to a few key performance indicators – too much data will slow you down and take too much time to collect. The recommendation is to measure a maximum of five things – Safety (such as OSHA rate or number of incidents), Quality (usually expressed in errors per given number of opportunities), Delivery (if you are getting things to your customers when promised), Productivity (such as units per labor hour), and morale (attendance and turnover data). The first metric tells you if your processes are able to be executed in a reasonably safe manner. The second tells you if your processes are being executed with the requisite level of quality. The third tells you if you are delivering value in a timely manner. The fourth tells you if your processes are being executed efficiently. The fifth tells you if your employees are engaged and reliable.

All five measures are important! Particularly in a Lean setting, you want to avoid just "focusing on the numbers" – usually this refers to total output or possibly efficiency (or both). Instead, you want to ensure that you can achieve your business objectives in terms of volume while also performing safely, with high quality, at the right time, and without running your team into the ground. So measuring all five is an important part of Lean management.

How To Do It
- *Define goals*

First, you need to define your goals. Safety goals are usually determined by your corporate risk department. Of course, most companies will tell you that the goal is to have no accidents. For quality, your business likely has a predefined acceptable level of quality, such as the common six-sigma goal of 250 DPMO (defects per million opportunities). Productivity can be engineered, observed, or just tribal knowledge to start with. For example, you might know through tribal knowledge that your storers are capable of 6 stores per hour. This would be a good number to start with for your goal. Attendance and turnover targets are also usually highly individualized by industry and site, and are likely determined by your HR group.

- *Create a board*

Once you know what your goals are, create a board that shows how your team is performing each hour. Below is a sample production or "pitch" board. There is a place for each operator to record their hourly performance, and a place for the leader to tally up the hourly and cumulative totals.

	Jane		Joe		Jeri		Jeff		Total	
	Goal	Actual	Goal	Actual	Goal	Actual	Goal	Actual	Goal	Actual
1	6	5	6	6	6	8	6	7	24	26
2	6	5	6	4	6	8	6	6	24	23
3	6	6	6	7	6	4	6	8	24	25
4	6	5	6	8	6	7	6	8	24	28
5	6	7	6	4	6	4	6	7	24	22
6	6	6	6	4	6	6	6	8	24	24
7	6	6	6	5	6	4	6	5	24	20
8	6	5	6	5	6	5	6	7	24	22
									192	190

- *Track hourly performance*

Notice in the picture above that performance is tracked by each employee by hour, and the total for the team by hour. This is not usually feasible for safety or morale, which are measured by the total for the day – assuming you are not having hourly safety incidents! Employees should update their own performance by hour; this lets them see their own performance in the context of overall team performance. Letting your employees know how they are performing is an essential part of Lean management! Traditionally, the Team Lead ensures the board is being filled out properly and lists the cumulative team performance hourly. As Supervisor, your role is to check the board by the hour and initial off every hour.

- *Adjust as needed*

The purpose of reviewing the board is two-fold. First, it ensures that you are aware of your team's performance, and second, it allows you to make adjustments based on what you observe.

- Individual performance

Take a moment to look at the example above. You will notice that one employee, "Joe", had five hours of performance below goal. No other team member had this low of performance. This would be a good opportunity to speak with Joe about his performance, and watch him work to see if there is any waste in his execution of the standard process.

- Team performance

Overall, the team was just below goal. If you observe that the team is consistently below goal and all the operators are functioning at about the same rate, then you will want to observe the entire process. It may be that your performance goal is unreasonable; chances are, however, that there is some waste built into the habits of all your operators. Use the **"Ohno circle"** or similar exercise to observe key parts of the process and look for waste that can be removed.

What is the Ohno Circle?

Taiichi Ohno was a famous Lean leader in Japan who came up with many of the tools we use today. One of these tools is the "Ohno Circle". This method is very simple: draw a circle on the floor with chalk and stand in it. Now observe everything you see, specifically looking for waste. It is amazing what you notice when you aren't allowed to wander!

Regular Accountability

Remember the dashboard example from above? Well, it only works if you use it! To drive consistent results, you also have to have a plan for *how* you use it. Imagine that you are on a road trip, and only check the dashboard when you feel like it. You might get halfway to Perth Amboy and run out of gas, or forget to check your speed and end up with a hefty ticket or fine. If your road trip takes several days, you will want to review your dash at the end of each day to take stock on how far you've come, your fuel levels, etc., so that you can adjust your travel plan for the next day as necessary. In the same way, you need to have structured daily meetings to review your team's performance and make adjustments as necessary.

Lean speaks of this habit as "Regular Accountability". Regular accountability is the habit of reviewing the team's performance on a regular basis. There are three levels of accountability that should happen on a daily basis; more meetings than this might be required, but it is very difficult to run your business with less than three.

Tier 1

This meeting is held between the Team Leads and hourly employees every day to assess the previous day's performance and share the game plan for the day. Problems in executing from the previous day should be brought to light in this meeting. Remember, "problems" should be defined in terms of waste in the process. The team needs to avoid judgmental language, or blaming other team members for challenges. If an employee "messes up", there is always a reason – it is this reason that should be uncovered and resolved. In the section on visual management, the entire team would have made their goal if Joe had performed according to expectation. However, saying as much in a team meeting is detrimental to team cohesion – imagine how that would make Joe feel. Instead, the communication should focus on the issues Joe faced that prevented him from performing. In fact, Joe's name shouldn't even be mentioned in the startup. Any correction to Joe should be in private. Remember, "praise in public, redirect in private".

Tier 2

This meeting is held between the Team Leads and Supervisors every day. This meeting is used to review the shift plan and adjust labor as necessary based on attendance. It is also an opportunity to coach the Team Leads on various aspects of their performance or current business needs.

Tier 3
This meeting is held between the Supervisors and the OM on a daily basis. This meeting is similar to the Tier 2, and allows the OM to make operational decisions based on the feedback from the Supervisors on their attendance or other issues.

What is a Tier Meeting?

The "tier" model is a way of looking at management that recognizes different levels in the organization. Tier 1 is always the level of the organization at which value is created. An easy way to look at this is Tier 1 "does the work". Tier 2 is the level that oversees Tier 1, and Tier 3 is the level that oversees Tier 2. The benefit of the "tier" model, is that it doesn't matter what job titles you use - the idea is easy to understand independent of labels. Tier 1 and the Tier 1 meeting are the most important parts of your business, as these are the people who actually do the work of the business.

How To Do it
- *Write out a meetings plan*

Start by writing out Who, What, When, and Where – who needs to be at each Tier meeting, what will be covered (this should already have been defined when you set your metrics), when the meetings will be held, and where they will be held (meetings should happen at the visual management board, to make it easy to review performance). Below is a general script to follow for Tier meetings:
1. Safety – review yesterday's results; share a safety message for the day
2. Quality – review yesterday's results; share a quality message for the day
3. Delivery – review yesterday's results and set today's goal
4. Productivity – review yesterday's results and set today's goal
5. Morale – review yesterday's results and share any HR announcements

You may have a safety and quality team that can provide daily messages; if not, consider asking team members to contribute by sharing a thought about how to work safely or a quality issue to be aware of. If you didn't meet your goals in a given category, ask the team what we can do differently today to meet the team's goals.

- *Lead first, then observe*

You'll want to execute the first few Tier meetings while your Team Lead learns how to do it well. But sooner or later, you'll need you Team Lead(s) to step up and lead the Tier 1 meeting. However, you should observe your Team Lead's meetings in order to provide helpful coaching. Remember what we said about Leadership earlier, and avoid any approach that comes across as paternalistic or judgmental.

- *Keep notes*

Take brief notes on your LSW about what was said in the meeting, and then compare those notes to the team's performance results at the end of the day. If you didn't get what you want, ask yourself if the meeting set the team in the proper direction. Often, lack of performance results can be traced back to not providing the team with good direction at the beginning of the shift.

Chapter Two Recap

The Four Pillars of LEAN are: Standard Work, Leader Standard Work, Visual Management, and Regular Accountability

Standard Work is: Doing the same task the same way every time

Standard Work requires: A documented process, training the employees, and observing their behaviors to ensure they are following the standard

Leader Standard Work is: A set of actions that a leader needs to accomplish every day in order to run the business consistently

Leader Standard Work requires: A document or checklist of activities, easy access (on your person), periodic review and adjustment

Visual Management is: The process of making your team's performance visible at a glance

Visual Management requires: A board or display area, periodic updates, periodic reviews

Regular Accountability is: The habit of reviewing team performance at regularly scheduled intervals

Regular Accountability requires: A written meetings plan, team contribution and interaction, observation and coaching

Chapter 3

Getting Things Done

Three Methods for Getting Things Done
Executing Your Deliverables
Effective Delegation

Three Methods for Getting Things Done

One issue that new Supervisors often face is how to get things done. Initially, this might sound odd – after all, the whole point of a Supervisor's job is to get things done. However, there are a couple of pitfalls that all leaders face that you need to watch out for from the get-go. *First*, it is almost a certainty that you will end up with more to get done than you can accomplish in any given day. *Second*, different objectives require one of three levels of execution – just doing something, teaming up with your direct reports to do something, or teaming up with a cross-functional team to get something done. Each of these levels requires different tactics. *Third*, different people in your organization are going to ask you to get things done, and probably won't stop until you tell them that you are booked.

Consider the following scenario. You show up for work, and have your regular duties to attend to – you have your LSW ready, you have a few notes for the daily meetings, and you know what your team needs to produce to win this day. On top of that, you are in the process of creating and implementing visual management on your shipping dock by taping staging lanes down. Your boss pops in and lets you know that the daily forecast doesn't include a special project, and that you need to pick three employees to help with a special repacking request. You quickly add that to your list, and find an email in your inbox from HR about an upcoming company picnic to announce to your team. You gather your notes to head out to the floor, and the Safety Manager stops you to let you know that he has some concerns with your taping plan for the dock. You have just taken on all three levels of task – things you can just do (HR memo), things that you can do with your team (special repack assignment), and things that require working with other departments (safety concern on dock taping). How will you accomplish them?

David Allen's book *Getting Things Done*[1] describes three possible directions we can take when presented with tasks to accomplish. When faced with more things than you can get done, David recommends sorting tasks into three categories. If you can just do something, just do it. If you can't just do it, delay the action – this might look like making a note on your LSW for future follow up commitment. In the example above, you may want to let the Safety Manager know that you don't have time to discuss with him today, but that you are going to delay any taping until you talk to him – and set a meeting time for Wednesday morning. There are some tasks, however, that can be delegated to others to accomplish. In the example above, the HR announcement could be given to your Team Lead to announce in the Tier 1 meeting.

In our example scenario, you received three different type of tasks, and you used all three tactics to get things done. The HR announcement was something you can do on your own, and you used the "delegate" method. The special repack project was something you could do with your team of direct reports, and you chose the tactic of "do" – this is what you will focus your personal energy on today. The dock taping is a task that requires collaboration with people outside of your direct reports, and you chose the "delay" tactic to manage this deliverable.

4Ds of time management

#1 DROP certain unimportant tasks

#2 DELEGATE work that is not necessary for you to do

#3 DELAY work that is not needed immediately

#4 DO what is essential & what adds the most value

---

[1] David Allen, *Getting Things Done*, (New York: Penguin Books), 2001.

How to Do It
- *Uncover the Problem*

In order to make a good decision on what to do, delay, or delegate, you will need to ask a few important questions when people come to you with tasks to accomplish. Ask enough questions find out what the *problem* is. The "problem" is the reason for the request, and what you are solving for. It can often be quite different from the request or requirement that you are being asked to fulfil. This happens because many people confuse *what they want solved* with *how to solve it*. Consider the following exchange:

"Hey, Shanice, at the end of the shift, can you make sure all your operators park their forklifts in G room?" (This is your boss talking).

"Sure thing, Bob! Have we been losing forklifts or something?" (Probing question – what is the actual problem?)

"Oh, no, nothing like that, it's just that our operators are parking their trucks near the time clock and it's getting cluttered and unsafe." (Here the boss reveals the actual problem.)

"Oh, ok Bob; I get it. We'll make sure the lifts get parked in G room."

At this point, you know what the actual problem is. It isn't just that trucks are being parked in the wrong area; it is that the trucks are being parked in the wrong way.

- *Find out what the deliverable is*

Second, find out what the deliverable is. In the example above, the deliverable is more than just parking in the G room; it is parking in a safe and tidy manner. This is important, because you could set yourself up for a situation where your employees do park in the G room, but park in a cluttered or unsafe way! Again, the deliverable is not always clearly stated, and without a few simple questions in the example above, you could end up not getting the desired results.

- *Assess your findings*

Once you know the problem and deliverable(s), you can make a better assessment of which tactic to use. You can assess a task by running it through the "important/urgent" matrix. In general, the more *important* a task is, the more important it is for you to execute it yourself rather than delegate it. In general, the more *urgent* a task is, the more important it is to do now, rather than delay.

Executing Your Deliverables

When the United States Air Force decided to bomb Afghanistan, they loaded up B2 Spirit bombers in Missouri, flew them halfway around the world (with multiple mid-air refuelings), delivered their payload, and returned safely to base in the heartland of the United States. This is probably a much more complex, dangerous, and high-stakes project than anything you will ever do at work! And yet, the Air Force has been executing this play successfully countless scores of times. So what is their secret sauce – what tool do they use to ensure flawless execution of such a dangerous, high risk task? They use a checklist. Yep, that's right; the humble checklist is the cornerstone of some of the most complex task execution in history.

This shouldn't surprise you, because a checklist is really just a form of standard work, as we discussed earlier. As well, we already introduced a checklist tool to you – your LSW. The key is to *use it*. When someone asks you to complete a task, *write it down*. Your LSW should include space to write out tasks and track them to closure.

As well, your LSW provides a very valuable tool for negotiating with other stakeholders – when someone asks you to do something, you can show them your LSW and let them know how busy you are – ask them which tasks should be prioritized, and which ones should be delayed.

Consider the following exchange:
"Hey Shanice," (Your boss again – Bob is a needy guy.)
"Hey, Bob, what's up?"
"Yeah, I have these TPS reports that I need you to get done today."
"Ok, that sounds important," (It doesn't sound important to you, but it sounds like it is important to Bob – take the other person's perspective). "Let me show you what I have on my plate." (Pulls out LSW)
"So it looks like today I have the steering committee meeting, the MPQ redesign kaizen event, and the LSW review committee meeting. It takes me about an hour to run TPS reports, so which of these other tasks would you like me to not get done today?"
"Oh, man, I didn't realize how busy you were. You know what, Shanice? I think I can give this to Jordyn; your other tasks are more important. Thanks though!"
This lets Bob know what your work load is and allows him to make an intelligent decision about how he wants to use his resources. This is another tactic for "managing up".

How to Do It

- *Write requests down*

When someone asks you to execute a task, write it down. You already have an LSW that outlines important deliverables to run your business consistently; use a section of your LSW as a checklist to track additional task requests as they come up.

- *Assess your workload*

As you are given additional tasks, assess these requests and figure out what you can and can't get done. Use the "important/urgent" matrix to decide what to do, what to delay, and what to delegate.

- *Communicate up, down, and across*

Once you know what you can and can't accomplish and which tactics you intend to employee, communicate with relevant stakeholders in the organization. Some tasks will need to be communicated down to your direct reports, some will need to be communicated up, to your boss, and some will need to be communicated across, to your peers. Don't be afraid to ask for help.

The Eisenhower Decision Matrix

	Urgent	Not Urgent
Important	**Do** — Do it now.	**Decide** — Schedule a time to do it
Not Important	**Delegate** — Who can do it for you?	**Delete** — Elminate it

Effective Delegation

Don't be a hero! You can't get everything done yourself, and that requires you to learn the art and skill of delegation. One of the hardest things for new Supervisors to learn is how to effectively delegate. This is not because delegation is especially difficult, but because it is a learned skill. Delegation requires three simple but important elements. First, you have to know the *deliverable*. Remember when we talked about this earlier? When communicating a task to others, be sure to carefully define the deliverable.

Good: "Janice, I need you to share this communication from HSE with the team. Be sure they understand that they are not to park in the handicapped spot unless they have a pass, and ensure everyone signs the memo so we have a record of the communication."

Not good: "Hey Janice, can you share this memo with the team? I appreciate it."

The second important element of delegation is knowing whom you can trust. This ties back into our previous discussion of leadership. Hopefully, you have been spending time learning your team, and have a good idea of who is good at what.

The third important element of delegation is controls or limits. For example, you may be delegating the task of improving the break area for your employees. However, you shared the deliverables and chose the right employee, but you forgot to add that there is a $1,000 dollar budget, and that the project needs to be completed by the end of the week. As a result, the project isn't completed for a month, and your employee spent $10,000 on new refrigerators! This is not the outcome you were looking for.

Finally, once you delegate, focus on *results*, not *methods*. Everybody has different ways of doing things, and the whole point of delegation is to free up bandwidth for yourself. Remember that delegation is more than a tool to help you manage – it also allows those under you to develop and grow. Make sure to praise your employees when they execute a task, even if their execution isn't as good as what you think you could do. Reserve coaching for instances where the employee distinctly contradicted your instructions or failed to produce the deliverable.

How to Do It

- *Print out and use your LSW*

This is the checklist that you will use to ensure that all your tasks get done; for it to work you have to use it. Develop the habit of using the LSW to manage your day; I used to leave mine on top of my computer so I'd see it first thing when I got to work. A common method many companies use is to post your LSW in a clear sleeve outside your work area or desk; if your company allows it, this is a great way to develop the LSW habit.

- *When you are asked to do a task, write it down on your LSW*

This lets you track all deliverables in one handy spot. If you are overburdened, share your LSW with your boss and ask for help or advice. Next to the task, write down which tactic you are going to use – do, delay, or delegate. If the tactic is delay, be sure to write a time for future commitment.

- *Ask questions to get to the root of requests*

Ensure you are spending your time getting the right results when asked to do a task. Be careful how you record a task – don't assume that you will remember what you meant in a couple of days, or even a couple of hours.

- *Manage your tasks by doing, delaying, or delegating*

Make a decision on which tactic to use depending on *urgency* and *importance*. If you are getting a lot of urgent tasks, plan some time to root cause and find out – no operation can be successful it if stays in "fire fighting mode" all the time. You, your boss, and your peers may need to look at structural change if the majority of your tasks are urgent.

_____

Chapter Three Recap
The three tactics for execution are: Do (just do it yourself), Delegate (give the task to someone else to accomplish), or Delay (set up a future time to address the task)

The most powerful tool in the world is: A checklist! Use your LSW as a checklist to ensure you are tracking all special tasks to completion

Delegation is accomplished by: Clearly defining the deliverables and time frame for completion, selecting the right employee for the job, setting a clear time for review of outcomes, and rewarding the employee who successfully accomplishes the task

Chapter 4

Get Better Every Day

The Continuous Improvement Mindset
Eliminating the Eight Wastes
Measuring Outcomes and Limiting Reaction

The Continuous Improvement Mindset

One of the most expensive and beautiful gems you can buy is a diamond – in fact, it is a symbol of love around the world and is often used in engagement rings to express love and devotion. It may surprise you to learn that in its natural state a diamond is actually quite ugly! It takes quite a bit of painstaking work to turn that lump of stone into a beautiful, valuable object. In the same way, your operation is like a diamond in the rough – it takes quite a bit of painstaking work to improve! This chapter deals with what you can do right now to start "polishing your diamond".

One of the keys to successfully supervising an operation involves a fundamental change of mindset. Consider the following story: You have a check engine light on in your car, and so you take it to your mechanic. Your mechanic is sympathetic, but informs you that he is just going on vacation, but that you can fix the problem yourself. He lets you use all of his tools, his garage, and his manuals. Do you think you will be able to fix your car? Probably not. The reason is simple – your mechanic is more than a collection of tools and information! In the same way, just having Lean tools will not make your operation Lean; you need to have a Lean mindset. The primary difference in your mind as a Supervisor will be transitioning from binary thinking to continuous improvement thinking. Binary thinking tends to be our culture's most prevalent *paradigm* (framework for understanding what we see). Right and wrong, good and bad, left and right, up and down, green light and red light, stop and go...you get the picture. As a result, we often look at our operation and outcomes in terms of good or bad. This is essentially the opposite of Lean thinking! Lean thinking adopts the mindset that we can always improve. Start now by coaching yourself – every day, your team is going to get a little bit better.

The continuous improvement model has two significant elements. The first is the idea that *systems* produce results. This is in sharp contrast to some "old school" management models that believe *people* produce results. Lean understands that people basically execute processes, and that examining and improving the process is the key to continuous improvement. The second significant element is that processes can be improved by removing waste. Lean defines eight wastes, which can be remembered pretty easily with the TIM WOODS acronym. TIM WOODS stands for transportation, inventory, motion, waiting, over-processing, overproduction, defects, and skill. Each of these represents a kind of waste that, by removing, can improve the process.

How to Do It

- *Create a Feedback Board*

Dedicate an area for your team to share ideas. Set aside time once a week with the team to review these ideas and decide which ones the team will take action on.

- *Create a Change Champions Team*

Enlist enthusiastic early adopters to help you implement the improvements the team identifies

- *Re-examine Your Processes*

Now that you understand the difference between a Continuous Improvement mindset and a binary mindset, take the time to re-examine all your processes and think through how things you might have considered "bad" in the past are opportunities for improvement

Eliminating the Eight Wastes

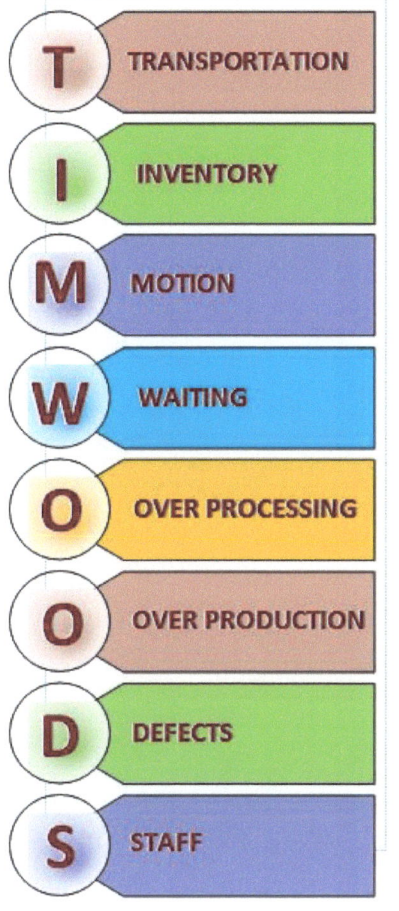

Transportation – every time material is transported, it is waste. Reducing transport distance or time can improve your process.

Inventory – inventory is waste; it represents resources (labor and materials) that you are not getting paid for. Lean CI seeks to reduce the amount of inventory needed on hand to keep processes running productively.

Motion – this refers to the motion of human bodies while performing their tasks. Setting up work stations to minimize motion will improve your processes.

Waiting – every minute spent waiting in order to execute a process is wasted labor. Not only are you paying someone to be idle, but you are missing out on the production they could be producing while they wait!

Overprocessing – this refers to creating more value than your customer is willing to pay for. An example might be overpacking a product that comes from the factory already packed for shipping. This is an unnecessary addition that adds cost without actually improving customer experience.

Overproduction – if a job produces more output than the next job can handle, you will end up with a stack of inventory in between processes. This is waste.

Defects – defects not only eat up time and resources that could be spent producing good product, they also end up having to be corrected! Reducing defects is a great way to improve your processes.

Skill – this refers to wasting the skill an employee might have. For example, if you have a trained welder picking parts, you are wasting his welding skill.

The key to shining in your role as a Supervisor is to change your mindset from thinking in terms of good or bad, and instead train yourself to believe that any process can be improved in small, incremental steps. You can do this by looking for these wastes in your processes and removing them. This is likely something that will require partnering with your boss, your quality group, and other stakeholders.

In order to move forward with your new found paradigm, you must also take the time to break old habits. People are often surprised to learn that one of the foundations to continuous improvement is to *stop doing stuff*. What do I mean by that? Well for starters, remember the five "C"s — Continual Change Creates Constant Confusion! If you come out to the floor every day looking to change things, you might create a culture where employees are unsure of how to do their job, and standard work is no longer being followed. Instead, you should have a structured plan for continuous improvement. Consider that there are many stakeholders in your organization, and they all probably have opinions about how things should be done. If you react to all these requests, you are likely to create a culture of the five Cs! Instead, you should have defined triggers and processes for implementing change that you and your boss agree on.

How to Do It

- *Post the Eight Wastes*

Put a list of the eight wastes on your Tier 1 board and encourage your team members to start recognizing them.

- *Utilize the Ohno Circle*

We discussed the "Ohno Circle" earlier as a tool for observing waste – write out a list of the eight wastes, stand in the circle, and start trying to recognize the eight wastes. This will help you to start learning to identify these wastes quickly.

- *Train to the Eight Wastes*

Train your employees to recognize the eight wastes as well. You can share the Ohno Circle exercise with them, but there are other tools you can use to encourage your employees. For example, you might have a pop quiz at the Tier 1, and whoever can name the most wastes gets an award.

- *Integrate with your idea board*

In the section on adopting a continuous improvement mindset, we suggested creating an employee idea board where your team can start suggesting improvement ideas. Teach your team to present their ideas in terms of eliminating one or more of the eight wastes.

Measuring Outcomes and Limiting Reaction

Some of the more effective triggers that you can adopt are "control limits" for your processes. Control limits can be carefully calculated by your engineering group, but aren't necessary to begin using this tool to help you control meaningful change. A control limit is nothing more than a level of performance that triggers *reaction* on your part. For example, imagine that you just started a new supervisor job. Your employees are currently producing at 100 units per hour. Your boss informs you that your team needs to operating at 125 units per hour. At this point, you would observe your processes for the wastes described above, and look for waste to remove from the processes. This is a proactive, Lean CI approach to managing your business. However, you should have a set threshold, or floor – a control limit – that triggers action if your team falls below a certain level. In the example above, you might set your lower control limit at 90 units per hour. If your team falls below this number, it triggers an investigation and subsequent action. This ties in to the production boards that we discussed earlier – the production board is a visual management tool that can define for you when there is a problem that you need to act on. The power of this approach is that it allows you to focus on proactively improving the processes unless a critically low output is reached. This helps to keep the operation out of fire-fighting mode. Remember, a control limit *prevents you* from spending time on reactionary tasks unless a certain agreed upon limit is breached.

An engineer can help you calculate control limits, but if you are setting your own limits based on your knowledge of the operation consider that all processes have a certain amount of variance. In the example above, consider that in any given week your team might average 100 units per hour, but one day they hit 90 and another day they hit 110.

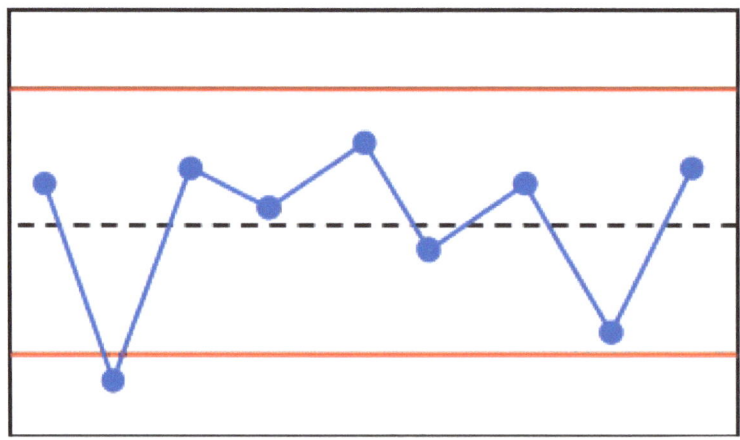

This is process variance. The point is that the lower control limit should be below this regular variance. If you hit 90 on a few days every week and still hit your weekly average of 100, then you shouldn't set your control limit "action trigger" at 90 or above. Perhaps 85 would be a better limit. Now imagine that you take this approach, and your boss pulls you aside the next week. She explains that she misspoke earlier, and the weekly average doesn't need to be 100, rather, that is the minimum that the team can hit every day to be successful. What she is really telling you is that your lower control limit needs to be 100! If you experience this, as I have, then you need to move the production goal *up* to compensate. In the example above, the minimum production in a successful week is 90, which is 10 units below goal. So if your new lower control limit is 100, then you would want to set your production goal at 110. At this point, you would also want to have a conversation with your boss to let her know what wastes you have observed in the processes, and what your plan is to bring average productivity up from 100 to 110. Remember, the point of having a control limit is to keep you focused on proactive leadership unless absolutely necessary. Your team might be having a down day or even week, but unless you are below your control limit, you don't need to spend time and energy investigation "what went wrong". Instead, you should be focused on how to make it a little bit better. Keep in mind that this must be a firm agreement with your boss. In the event that your selected control limit is not meeting the needs of the business, consider setting new control limits periodically – for example, on Mondays. If control limits are adjusted too frequently, you lose the benefit! The point is to reduce the amount of reactionary energy spent in the operation.

> **Technical Point**
>
> *This section is a bit more technical than the rest of the book. If it is a little dificult to understand, don't worry about it. The basic idea is that you need a performance limit that tells you when the processes is unhealthy and requires immediate attention. On the other hand, if you haven't hit this limit, you want to avoid wasting energy reacting to less than optimal results, since all processes have some ups and downs.*

Once you are comfortable with this idea, consider that you can also implement *upper* control limits. While common in manufacturing where out of tolerance product is bad regardless of magnitude, upper control limits are sometimes ignored in other contexts. This is a shame, because upper control limits can also help your operation out. In the preceding example, it is normal for your team to operate between 90 and 110 average unit output. But what if your team produces 125 units? Well, in this case you might want to do an investigation to find out not what went *wrong*, but what went *right*. After all, you want more days of 125 unit production, right? Setting an upper control limit gives you a visual trigger to investigate *positive* results, and find out what happened so you can replicate success in the future. An upper control limit can also help you uncover real problems – consider for a moment if your team increased productivity by skipping a crucial step in the process! An upper control limit triggers you to look into this so you can correct the issue and bring the process back to standard.

How to Do It

- *Break your span of control into chunks*

You already learned how to define your responsibilities as a series of processes. Look at the processes and floor layouts to rationally divide your area of responsibility into manageable "chunks". For example, you might be the Shipping Supervisor. As such, you are responsible for picking orders, getting them packed, getting trailers loaded, and getting drivers off the lot with full loads. This already shows you four good chunks you could break your responsibility down into. As well, each of these functions probably has its own production board or visual management tool (or will, once you implement earlier parts of this book!). By breaking your work down into chunks, it makes it easier to focus on sustaining small improvements. Once you gain some skill in managing continuous improvement, you will be able to drive initiatives in several area of the business at once, but for starters, just focus on improving one piece at a time.

- *Establish metrics and control limits*

You already learned how to do this, now it is time to use it. *Metrics* allow you to measure actual improvements gained from your efforts. *Control limits* allow you to avoid reactionary action unless the business actually calls for it. Each "chunk" of your business should have its own metrics and control limits, and these should be visually managed on some type of board. Remember, you don't have to spend a lot of money or get fancy with visual management! A dry erase board or even paper stapled to an old-fashioned cork board is more than enough to get you going in the right direction.

- *Work on one chunk at a time*

Select one area to focus on, and make a small change. Then measure the results. For example, you may choose to focus on order picking first. You measure productivity, and then use the Ohno circle (see the next section) to observe waste. You discover that by moving the order drop off zone, you can reduce travel time. Make the change, using the change management and leadership lessons already covered, and then measure your results. If you see an improvement, move on to the next chunk of your business.

- *Utilize the Ohno circle*

The Ohno circle refers to a method for observing the seven wastes. It looks like this – pick a circle to stand in in your operation. Now just stand there for 30 minutes and mark down every type of waste you see. You might be astonished by just how much you can observe in 30 minutes! An alternative method for mobile operations, such as order picking, is to follow several pickers and look at common wastes or barriers that different operators share. This is different from a process observation because you are not looking for process compliance, but rather are looking for the seven wastes. The more operators experience the same waste, the more likely that removing it will move the needle forward.

So what if you make a change and don't see an improvement? Well, don't worry about it! If you eliminated waste, you will see benefit eventually. Move on to the next opportunity.

Chapter Four Recap

The CI Model is: A fundamental change of mindset (paradigm shift). It moves away from thinking about your business in terms of right and wrong or good and bad, and moves toward thinking about it in terms of steady, daily improvement. It does this by identifying and eliminating waste in the operation

The Seven Wastes are: Transportation, Inventory, Motion, Waiting, Overprocessing, Overproduction, Defects, and Skills

The CI mindset includes: Taking the time to stop doing old habits that conflict with your new paradigm

Limit reactionary energy by utilizing control limits: Control limits set clear boundaries for taking reactionary measures. This frees up your time to focus on your proactive continuous improvement strategy

Chapter 5

Conflict Resolution

The Conflict Resolution Model
Cognitive, Emotional, and Behavioral Elements
What if They Just Say No

The Conflict Resolution Model

Chances are, you haven't heard of Moshe Dayan. He was an Israeli general and statesman in the twentieth century who was famous for his menacing eye patch and penchant for rebellion. In fact, as a teenager he was imprisoned by the ruling British authorities for joining a nascent militia group! His career was pockmarked with success and failure, but he is perhaps most famous for negotiating a peace treaty between Israel and Egypt at the Camp David Accords – an accomplishment which garnered him national fame, but also expulsion from his conservative Labor Party. Despite the volcanic political climate of the time, Dayan has gone down in history as an expert negotiator and guru in conflict resolution.

Moshe Dayan was caught in a very emotional dilemma. On the one hand, Egypt had legitimate grievances about Israel, and presented a clear and present danger to Israel's security as a nation. On the other hand, many factions within Israel were not interested in recognizing Egypt's grievances. Dayan knew that the future security of his nation was at least partially dependent upon a peace agreement with their neighbor. Astonishingly, Dayan was able to negotiate a peace that saw Israel withdraw troops and civilians from the Sanai peninsula in exchange for peace with Egypt. The entire history of the Middle East was changed through his ability to de-escalate conflict between Egypt and Israel, as well as friction within Israel's government itself. While you will not face the same high stakes or level of complexity that Moshe Dayan did, you will still face conflict in the workplace, and need to develop your skills at conflict resolution to be the best Supervisor that you can be.

One of the important tools you need in your toolbelt as a Supervisor is the ability to resolve conflict. It is important to understand from the get-go – you will experience conflict in your job, and need to learn how to resolve it effectively. You will have employees who challenge your authority (you may have even been "that guy" once!), you will have employees argue with other employees, and you will likely have to share and enforce company policies that are unpopular. *This is ok*. It is a normal part of life, and you can do it! In fact, families do this all the time, and chances are that you already have some experience resolving conflict. Do you have a toddler? Well then, I guarantee you have some conflict resolution experience!

Remember, as a Supervisor, you are a *leader*. People look to you to provide guidance and boundaries. You should strive to create a culture where your employees are comfortable expressing disagreements and grievances but know how to do it in a professional way. One way you can empower this kind of healthy culture is by developing your ability to resolve conflict in a meaningful way. For the next scenario, imagine that you are the employee. Your Supervisor has just informed the team that anyone late to the startup meeting will be considered late, no matter what time they punched in. You don't think this is fair, because you have been clocking in on time for months and then going to your locker to prepare for your shift. You might be a few minutes late to the startup meeting, but who cares? It's not such a big deal. You approach your supervisor...
"Man, this is bull crap! You expect me to clock in early now?"

Consider the following four responses from your Supervisor:

 "Well this is the way we are doing it now, so starting tomorrow ensure you are at the meeting on time."

"Oh Jerry, I know. But 'corporate' says we have to do it this way. I know it sucks."

"Excuse me? I'm the Supervisor. You can either fall in line or get a write up!"

"Uh...I just remembered I have a meeting to go to. I'll discuss with you later."

How would you feel if your Supervisor responded in any of these ways? Probably not very good! As a Supervisor, you can respond to conflict like this in a meaningful way by following a few simple steps, which we will review in the "How to do it" section. This chapter is unique, in that all three sections will be pulled together into a single "how to do it" section at the end.

In the meantime, it is important to recognize the model of conflict resolution that we are dealing with at work. Psychologists discuss several different models of conflict or dispute resolution. The branch of conflict resolution that we are dealing with is primarily the "dual model" – two individuals having a disagreement. This is different from more complex conflict that might involve groups of people or even entire nations. Luckily, you don't have to be a United Nations diplomat to be successful at work! In the dual model, there are generally five different approaches. The first is *avoidance*. We saw this above when your fictional Supervisor responded "Uh…I just remembered I have a meeting to go to. I'll discuss with you later." This is not an effective conflict resolution method for Supervisors. Your team is looking to you for leadership and guidance.

The second approach is *yielding*. This is where you yield your demands to the other party. In general, this is not a tactic available to you as a Supervisor – if you make an exception for one employee, you have to make an exception for all!

The third approach is competitive or combative. This is exemplified in the third response in our fictional encounter, "Excuse me? I'm the Supervisor. You can either fall in line or get a write up!" This kind of approach is guaranteed to alienate your team and create a toxic culture.

The fourth approach is *conciliation*. This is a bargaining or compromising style, and you may be able to use it sometimes as a Supervisor.

The final tactic is the *cooperation* style. This style is characterized by cooperating with the other party by showing concern for their wellbeing while still enforcing the requirement. This is the most common method that you will use in your job as a Supervisor.

As you experience conflict as a leader, think about what you are hearing in these terms, and be intentional about which tactic is appropriate in the situation. The cooperation style is very effective, and you should try to use it whenever possible.

Cognitive, Emotional, and Behavioral Elements

There are three "resolutions" that you need to understand to effectively resolve conflict – cognitive, emotional, and behavioral. Cognitive resolution is the way we mentally understand the conflict. Emotional resolution is how we feel about the conflict. Behavioral resolution is how we act, or behave, post conflict. In the responses above, we see imbalanced responses that only focus on one aspect of conflict resolution.

"Well this is the way we are doing it now, so starting tomorrow ensure you are at the meeting on time."
This response only deals with cognitive resolution – you are essentially telling the employee the intellectual boundaries. Chances are, they already understand this! They just don't agree with it, which is why they are objecting.

"Oh Jerry, I know. But 'corporate' says we have to do it this way. I know it sucks."
This response reinforces and validates the employee's negative emotions. This is very unhealthy. Although the employee has a right to be upset about a policy, your job is to be a champion of company policy. If possible, you should help the employee to emotionally connect with the policy, even if it causes hardship. Remember, humans are whole people; while we may wish people would accept direction on the basis of logic alone, this is rarely the case.

"Excuse me? I'm the Supervisor. You can either fall in line or get a write up!"
This response deals entirely with behavior – shape up or ship out! This is a great way to get employees to hate you. While you will ultimately need a change in behaviors, ignoring the cognitive and emotional aspects of conflict resolution is ineffective.

"Uh…I just remembered I have a meeting to go to. I'll discuss with you later."
This response doesn't deal with the conflict at all – it simply avoids it. Clearly this is not a way to gain respect as a Supervisor!

What if They Just Say No?

There is one last type of conflict to consider. This is when an employee just tells you "no". Consider the following exchange:

"Hey Jerry, I need you to help Janice clean up the fab area. Can you grab the sweeper and head over there?"
"Man, that's not my job!"

In these cases, follow these three steps:
1. Restate the request and ask the employee to clarify their response.
   "Jerry, I'm asking you to help clean up the shipping dock. Are you telling me that you aren't going to do this?"

2. Get a witness.
   If at this point the employee still refuses to do as asked, get a fellow Supervisor as a witness and repeat step two. Try to keep this low key. You need a witness to verify the employee's response and ensure you aren't misunderstanding, but the point is not to intimidate the employee. Remember, if the employee complies at this point, you will have to work with they for the foreseeable future, so be aware of how your approach makes the employee feel. You don't want to create an awkward future through lack of skill.

3. Follow site policy.
   If at this point the employee still refuses to follow your instructions, follow the policy for dealing with direct disobedience set up by your HR department.

Remember, we are all grown individuals, and as such, we have the right to make our own choices. Don't waste time or emotional energy judging another individual's choice. Sometimes it can be easy to take direct disobedience as a lack of respect or a personal attack on us as a leader. Try to avoid this kind of thinking. Not everything is about you, and it doesn't really change anything even if it is. Your job is to run the business, and hopefully develop employees to positively contribute to the common cause. But sometimes people choose not to. That is okay. You can't force them and they will have to bear the consequences of their choice, whatever that might be.

Keep in mind that direct disobedience is rare, and usually has underlying factors.
If the employee complies after step one or two, plan some time to follow up with the employee and reinforce that you are regularly going to make this kind of request from them. Try to find out why they initially refused, and work to resolve the underlying issues. For example, the employee might just not want to do the work. In this case, explain that this is part of the work and ask what you can do to make it more tolerable. Perhaps you can implement some kind of game or contest to  make it more interesting. In other cases, you might find out that the employee is sore because they feel like they do more than their fair share of cleaning. Perhaps you realize that you don't have a fair or equitable way of distributing cleaning tasks. This is an opportunity for you to thank the employee for bringing this to your attention and commit to creating a cleaning plan or something similar to make the distribution of tasks more equitable.

Remember, the goal is to help and empower your team to succeed! The goal is not to enforce compliance or establish your authority as a Supervisor. Remember our discussion of leadership? You are looking to leverage social influence to gain aid and support! By combining your knowledge of leadership and conflict resolution, you create a powerful culture of positive reinforcement.

How to do it

- *Address the emotional, cognitive, and behavioral element*

Consider this alternative response to the example above, "Jerry, I understand that you're upset – we're changing the way we're doing things, and change is never easy. I'm not asking you to clock in early, I just need the team to be present at the startup meeting in a timely manner. There's a five minute window, so you should be able to do it. We share important information in the meeting which we don't want you to miss, and you wouldn't want the rest of the team waiting on you to get started. Starting tomorrow I expect everyone to be at the startup meeting on time, and if there is anything I can do to help you be there just let me know. I'm here to help. Can I count on you to be on time?"

Wow! What a difference from the other responses. Let's break down this response.

"Jerry, I understand that you're upset – we're changing the way we're doing things, and change is never easy." This addresses the emotional aspect. Recognize the employee's feelings and let him know that it is ok to have feelings! Your goal is to allow the employee to experience the emotional adjustment to change in a way that is positive and professional.

"I'm not asking you to clock in early, I just need the team to be present at the startup meeting in a timely manner. There's a five minute window, so you should be able to do it." This part of the response addresses the cognitive element – you are clarifying in the employee's mind what the actual new requirement is. You may have noticed that the employee's initial complaint replaced the actual facts of the requirement with an emotional substitute – you didn't ask the employee to clock in early, but this is his way of complaining. He may believe that clocking in early is the only way to fulfil the requirement, so you are correcting that assumption.

"Starting tomorrow I expect everyone to be at the startup meeting on time, and if there is anything I can do to help you be there just let me know. I'm here to help." This part of the response addresses the behavioral aspect of the conflict – it makes concrete what behavior you expect out of your employee. By using the phrase "everybody" instead of "you", you are subtly reminding the employee that this is not directed at this employee alone and that the whole team is being held to the same expectations.

- *Explain the benefits*

It isn't enough to just address the thee aspects of conflict, you must also explain the benefits and attempt to gain commitment from the employee. In the example above, the benefits to the employee and team are explained succinctly: "We share important information in the meeting which we don't want you to miss, and you wouldn't want the rest of the team waiting on you to get started." This serves two purposes. First, it lets the employee know the *why* behind the decision – this is an important part of leadership in general. Even if the employee is still angry with the new requirement, they at least know why the requirement is in place. The second part of this response is that it puts some social pressure on the employee to comply – if they are late, the rest of the team has to wait on them to arrive! This reminds the employee that they are part of a team.

- *Gain commitment*

Finally, it is usually appropriate to attempt to gain commitment from your employee as part of your conflict resolution. In the example above, you close the response with, "Can I count on you to be on time?" This reinforces your expectation and puts the ball in your employee's court. You've answered their objection, clarified expectations, offered your support, and now you are asking them to comply. Just be aware that many employees are not used to this approach, and might be unprepared to answer. As a result, you might get one of several responses.

"Pffft. Fine. Ok."

"I doubt it!"

"I mean, come on, man! This is garbage!"

Generally, the response will fall into one of three categories. The first is compliance – it might be grudging ("Pffft. Fine. Ok"), but basically they are agreeing to try. In this case, you can simply thank the employee and move on. Don't forget to smile! The second type of response is non-comital, but non-combative ("I doubt it!"). In these cases, the employee feels like they should be arguing their point, but has basically accepted that you are not going to budge on your expectations. In these cases it is often helpful to respond with something like, "I believe in you, Jerry! You can do it." The last example is combative or argumentative ("I mean, come on, man! This is garbage!"). In these cases, the best response is to simply say, "Well, Jerry, this is the new expectation. If there is anything I can do to help you deliver, just let me know." Remember, you will have to work with this employee for the foreseeable future. Treat them like you would want to be treated while still upholding your duties as a Supervisor.

Chapter Recap
Conflict resolution is: A normal, healthy part of life, leadership, and supervising

The three aspects or resolution that you need to address are: Cognitive, emotional, and behavioral

The most effective conflict resolution tactic is: Conciliation

When using the conciliation tactic, you should: Address emotional, cognitive, and behavioral conflict; explain the benefits; gain commitment.

Conclusion

I hope you found this book helpful, and as much fun to read as it was to write. Putting these skills into play rapidly can help you achieve the outcomes and goals you want. More importantly, these skills can help you make the world a better place, for you and for those you influence. I hope this is the beginning of a beautiful journey for you – a journey of skill, self-mastery, and business excellence.

Remember, a skilled leader is able to remain focused on business outcomes while leveraging social influence to enlist the aid of others in accomplishment of a common task. If you can master this discipline, there is nothing that can stop you. And that is my deepest wish for you.

About the Author

John Thacker is a logistics and supply chain professional with over two decades of experience in warehousing, logistics, transportation, and supply chain, specializing in the 3PL space. John has had the opportunity to work for and with *Fortune* 100 companies, large private enterprises, startups, and midsize businesses. John has an undergraduate from Pensacola Christian College, a Masters of Business Administration from the University of Louisville, and post-graduate courses in Supply Chain management from the Massachusetts Institute of Technology's Center for Transportation and Logistics. John is also a certified Black Belt in Lean Six Sigma. Throughout his career, John has thrived on respecting individuals, serving customers, and striving for excellence. John is a type eight and one on the enneagram, which is no surprise to those that work with him.

John currently resides in the Dallas, TX area with his wife and two children.

www.ingramcontent.com/pod-product-compliance
Lightning Source LLC
Chambersburg PA
CBHW042025150426
43198CB00002B/71